Reality Television

by Megan Kopp

Content Consultant
Max Dawson
nt Professor of Radio, TV, & Film
Northwestern University

CORE
LIBRARY

Printed in the United States of America,
North Mankato, Minnesota
112012
012013

THIS BOOK CONTAINS AT LEAST 10% RECYCLED MATERIALS.

Editor: Karen Latchana Kenney
Series Designer: Becky Daum

Cataloging-in-Publication Data
Kopp, Megan.
 Reality television / Megan Kopp.
   p. cm. -- (Hot topics in media)
Includes index.
ISBN 978-1-61783-735-7
1. Reality television programs. 2. Reality television programs--Social aspects. I. Title.
155.9--dc14

                                        2012946368

Photo Credits: Matt Sayles/AP Images, cover, 1; Sipa/AP Images, 4; Donald Traill/AP Images, 7; CBS Photo Archive/Getty Images, 10; Ron Galella, Ltd./WireImage/Getty Images, 12; Kristie Bull/AP Images, 15; Red Line Editorial, 17, 27; Monty Brinton/CBS/Getty Images, 18, 29; Michael N. Todaro/Getty Images, 23; Ray Tamarra/Getty Images, 24; Mark J. Terrill/AP Images, 30, 36, 45; Carlo Allegri/Getty Images, 32; Reed Saxon/AP Images, 35; Evan Agostini/AP Images, 39; Mel Evans/AP Images, 40

CONTENTS

CHAPTER ONE
What Is Reality Television? . . . 4

CHAPTER TWO
Exploding Reality 10

CHAPTER THREE
The Different Worlds
of Reality 18

CHAPTER FOUR
Effects of Reality 24

CHAPTER FIVE
Let's Get Real 32

Important Dates. 42

Stop and Think 44

Glossary. 46

Learn More. 47

Index 48

About the Author .48

What Is Reality Television?

Jennifer Lopez broke down in tears after the elimination of Chris Medina on *American Idol.* Emotions ran high when Kourtney Kardashian gave birth to daughter Penelope on the 2011–2012 season finale of *Keeping Up with the Kardashians.* And Blake Shelton was moved when his wife sung "The House That Built Me" on *The Voice* in 2011.

American Idol hopeful Chris Medina did not reach the end of the competition.

These three scenes have one thing in common: they are all examples of real-life emotion on reality television.

So what is reality television? Beyond emotion, it is entertaining nonfiction television. Generally, reality television shows do not use scripted dialogue. Scenes are shot as they happen, but they are heavily edited to make the final shows. These shows feature a range of participants, from average people to those with extraordinary abilities. Some are filled with people who want to become celebrities. And others feature models and actors. No matter who the participants are, there is almost always a mix of strong personalities.

The Numbers Are Real

Reality television is big. These numbers show just how popular these shows are:

- Fifty-one million people watched the first-season finale of *Survivor* in 2000.
- *American Idol* was the second most-watched television program in the 2011–2012 season.
- As of 2012, MTV's *Real World* is still on television 20 years after it first aired.

Khloe Kardashian, left, and Kim Kardashian are seen filming *Keeping Up with the Kardashians* on October 6, 2010, in New York City.

Reality television shows can be filled with emotional drama, humor, or crafty deceit. Often there is a contest involved. The shows can be set in ordinary places such as a house, as in *Big Brother*. They can also feature unusual places and situations. Reality TV has become a huge part of our popular culture.

Disorderly Reality

Extreme hoarding is a mental disorder. Hoarders fill up their living spaces with objects and garbage. The show *Hoarders* features hoarders in their living spaces. The show brings in professionals to treat the hoarders and clean up their living spaces.

In an interview in *Media Magazine*, reality television expert Professor Annette Hill discussed why people like this kind of show:

> *Firstly, it's . . . the fact that it is a mix of the things you like in other shows, a bit of soap opera, a bit of documentary, a bit of talk show. We're attracted to that hybrid nature of the genre.*
>
> *A second factor would be the emphasis on emotions, drama, relationships: our hopes and fears and dreams, and what makes us angry, what makes us cry, what makes us happy. . . . And we get to interact with these people, whether through arguing with them, relating to them, or voting for or against them.*

Source: Jenny Grahame. "Reality TV: An Interview with Annette Hill." Media Magazine. December 2009: 14–18. Web. Accessed October 22, 2012.

What's the Big Idea?

Take a close look at Hill's words. What is her main idea? What evidence is used to support her point? Come up with a few sentences showing how Hill uses two or three pieces of evidence to support her main point.

CHAPTER TWO

Exploding Reality

It all started with one man's goal to make people laugh. Allen Funt thought it would be fun to see how people reacted to silly jokes. In 1948 Allen Funt's show *Candid Camera* was a new idea.

The show used hidden cameras to film ordinary people faced with a set-up gag. In one prank a tiny car pulled into a gas station. Then the driver asked the attendant for a fill. The hidden camera captured the

One scene on *Candid Camera* revealed comedian Harpo Marx hidden inside a soda pop machine, surprising people when they bought a bottle.

The 1992 cast of *The Real World: New York* attended the MTV Video Music Awards that year.

attendant's amazement as the car took much more gas than expected. The trick was that there was a hidden tank in the trunk.

When the joke was revealed, it was always tagged with "Smile, you're on *Candid Camera*."

Many credit Funt's show as being the beginning of reality television.

A Popular Genre

Many reality shows followed *Candid Camera*. Audiences were soon glued to *Truth or Consequences, What's My Line, You Asked for It,* and *This Is Your Life.*

In 1973, *An American Family* was launched. The 12-hour documentary series followed a family named the Louds in their daily lives for seven months.

In 1992 MTV's *The Real World* changed reality television. Producers took seven very different people and put them in a New York City apartment. Then they let the cameras roll. Viewers never knew

Is There a Formula?

Reality television usually stars unique characters. The reality television genre depends on strong personalities. Would *American Idol* have been an instant hit without Simon Cowell? Donald Trump has as strong of a personality as the participants he looks to hire on *The Apprentice.* Producers look for characters that produce strong reactions from audiences.

what was going to happen next. No show had done this before. The network chose participants for the program, but it did not have a script.

Eight years later, *Survivor* became a surprise hit. The show averaged 28 million viewers per episode in its first two seasons. Reality television became shows that made big money for networks.

American Idol burst onto the small screen in 2002. It was the most watched TV series from 2005 to 2011, according to the Nielsen ratings. These ratings measure a show's audience size. It ranked first of all TV shows among adults (ages 18 to 49) for eight straight seasons. The 2012 *American Idol*

Reality around the World

Many reality shows popular in the United States began in Europe. These include:

- *Survivor*: Based on *Expedition Robinson,* a Swedish program
- *American Idol*: An offshoot of the United Kingdom's *Pop Idol*
- *Big Brother*: First aired in the Netherlands

Carrie Underwood has become a very successful musician since winning *American Idol* in 2005.

winner Phillip Phillips's single "Home" has sold more than 1 million copies. The 2002 *American Idol* winner, Kelly Clarkson, has sold more than 3.5 million copies of her single "Stronger." And the 2005 winner Carrie Underwood has sold just under 13.5 million albums.

Reality show stars make a lot of money on their shows. Some of the best paid reality stars are Gordon Ramsey on *Hell's Kitchen* and Christina Aguilera on *The Voice*. Both made more than $200,000 for each episode in 2012–2013. And *Jersey Shore* star Pauly D makes $175,000 an episode.

Reality shows have had great ratings. Each year, new kinds of reality shows appear on the air.

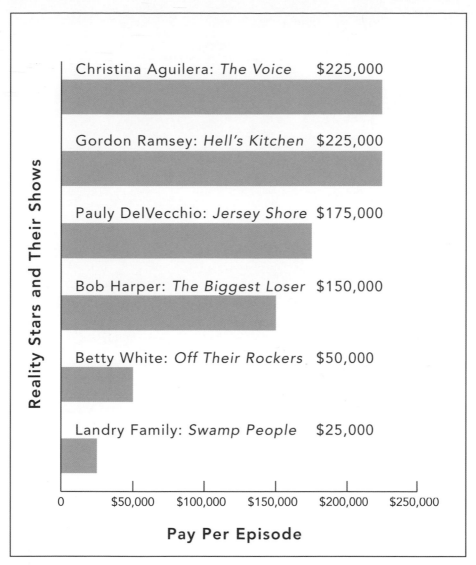

Christina Aguilera: *The Voice* $225,000

Gordon Ramsey: *Hell's Kitchen* $225,000

Pauly DelVecchio: *Jersey Shore* $175,000

Bob Harper: *The Biggest Loser* $150,000

Betty White: *Off Their Rockers* $50,000

Landry Family: *Swamp People* $25,000

Reality Stars and Their Shows

0     $50,000 $100,000 $150,000 $200,000 $250,000

Pay Per Episode

Reality Pays

This graph shows how much some reality stars were paid per episode in the 2012–2013 season. Take a look at this graph and compare it with the information in the text. How is this information similar? How is it different?

CHAPTER THREE

The Different Worlds of Reality

From game shows to makeovers, dating shows to talent competitions—there are many different types of reality programs. Most can be separated into one of five basic genres.

These five genres of reality television include:

- Adventure and competition-style game shows
- Makeover and self-improvement programs
- Talent-based shows

Host Jeff Probst with contestants of Survivor: South Pacific in 2011

Top Shows

In the 2011–2012 season, reality shows grabbed 10 of the top 30 spots in the ratings. Out of the 195 shows listed by *TV By The Numbers*, the top ten reality shows were:

2. *American Idol* performance show
3. *The Voice* performance show
6. *American Idol* results show
10. *X Factor* performance show
15. *X Factor* results show
16. *The Voice* results show
20. *Survivor: South Pacific*
28. *America's Got Talent* (Mondays)
29. *Survivor: One World*
30. *Dancing with the Stars*

- Reality humor shows
- Lifestyle and drama programs

Go Big or Go Home

Adventure and competition-style game shows such as *Survivor* and *Big Brother* film people competing to win a prize. Cast members must live together in a confined space. That space might be a beach or a house. One by one, cast members are voted off until one person remains. That person is the winner.

Dating shows include *The Bachelor* and *The Bachelorette.* Job search shows include *The Apprentice* and *America's Next Top Model.* They are other types of competition shows.

A New You

Makeover and self-improvement shows such as *Supernanny* and *The Biggest Loser* highlight a person or group of people changing their lives. Home renovation programs such as *Extreme Makeover: Home Edition* are another type in this genre. The change could be of the participants, their home environment, or the world around them.

These shows usually introduce the current situation and then follow the steps leading to a final change.

You've Got Talent

Talent shows such as *American Idol, So You Think You Can Dance,* and *America's Got Talent* follow a talent search format. Participants are also voted off until one person wins. These shows play up the interaction of the host or hosts with the reality stars. Many shows add interviews that tell the audience more about the reality star's personal life.

Ha, Ha, Humor

Hoaxes, jokes, and stunts gone wrong—it's all material for reality television. Shows such as *Punk'd* and *America's Funniest Home Videos* often involve hidden cameras.

Celeb-reality

Popular reality shows starring celebrities include *Keeping Up with the Kardashians*, *Celebrity Fit Club*, and *Dancing with the Stars*. Celebrities participate as themselves in their day-to-day lives, join in on a weight-loss or rehab program, or attempt to learn new skills such as ballroom dancing.

Living the Life

There's life as a deckhand on an Alaskan king crabbing boat in *Deadliest Catch*. Then there's life in a house stuffed to the rafters in *Hoarders*. In this type of show, cameras film an unusual lifestyle. If a

Film crews film *Jersey Shore* cast members Ronnie Ortiz-Magro, *back,* and Pauly D DelVecchio, *front,* in 2012.

person needs help, many shows offer ways to improve the person's life. Different lifestyles and drama are a big part of reality TV.

There is another type of lifestyle show that is purely social. More conflict and emotion is better for social lifestyle shows such as *Jersey Shore.*

CHAPTER FOUR

Effects of Reality

Is it possible to find true love in three weeks? Fairy-tale endings can happen. Trista Rehn beat the odds when she chose her groom, Ryan Sutter, on *The Bachelorette* in 2003. As of 2012 the couple was still happily married and had two children. On the set of *The Bachelor* in 2009, however, jaws dropped when Jason Mesnick dumped Melissa Rycroft for runner-up Molly Malaney. The success rate for on-air romance is

Trista Rehn and Ryan Sutter made a love connection on the reality show *The Bachelorette.*

very low. The list of failures is much longer than the number of fairy-tale endings.

Reality TV directly affects the people involved in the shows, but it can also have a surprising effect on viewers. Viewers often become emotionally invested in the outcome of the show.

Spin of the Reality Wheel

Starring on a reality show can bring fame and fortune. Just look at Carrie Underwood. After winning the fourth season of *American Idol*, she won several music awards.

On the flip side, winning a reality show can bring a lot of trouble. Richard Hatch won *Survivor*'s first season. But he ended up in jail for tax evasion. He did not pay taxes on the prize that he won on the show.

Negative Results

According to a 2009 Pew Research Center study, viewers mostly think reality television is a bad thing. Sixty-three percent said reality television coming on air was a change for the worse in the 2000s. Only 8 percent said it was a change for the better. Lying, cheating, and verbal abuse are common

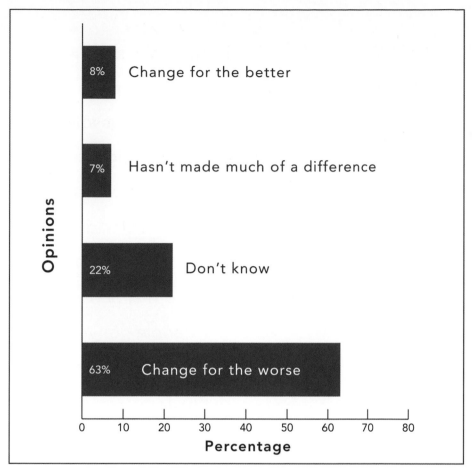

Opinions

8% Change for the better

7% Hasn't made much of a difference

22% Don't know

63% Change for the worse

0 10 20 30 40 50 60 70 80
Percentage

Opinions of Reality TV

A 2009 Pew Research Center study about technology and social change in the 2000s included opinions on reality television. The people who responded were asked if they thought reality television was a change for the better or worse in society. This graph shows the results. Look at how this information is shown in the graph. Compare it with the information in the text. How are they similar or different?

Kid Nation

In 2007 the reality show *Kid Nation* caused a lot of controversy. The contestants were 40 kids from ages 8 to 15. The kids were put in a New Mexico ghost town. The kids were given 40 days to build a town that worked. The kids had to cook their own meals, haul water, clean outhouses, run businesses, and create rules. Parents of the contestants were told that their children might be exposed to hazards causing injury or even death. The show was later canceled.

behaviors in many reality shows. One of the negative things about reality television is that it often gives a distorted view of the world. It can change what people think of as normal behavior.

People get yelled at on *The Apprentice*, or dumped on *The Bachelor*, or lied to on *Survivor*.

In a 2010 Brigham Young University study, researchers compared five reality shows and five non-reality shows for showing hurtful behavior. They found 52 acts of aggression per hour on reality TV. There were 33 per hour on the non-reality programs. Gossip, insults, and dirty looks are at the mild end of

Kids were the stars of the reality show *Kid Nation*.

the scale. Physical fights between the cast members are common on MTV's *Jersey Shore*. Most people don't think this affects them. But studies show that this meanness can rub off on viewers.

Positive Impacts

On the other hand, a study conducted by the Girl Scout Research Institute notes that although there are negative influences, reality TV can also have a positive impact. According to the study, girls who watch reality TV on a regular basis are more self-assured than those

America's Got Talent winner Bianca Ryan was only 11 years old when she won the show in 2006.

who don't watch these shows. Many of the reality TV fans wanted to become leaders and saw themselves as role models. The majority of regular reality TV viewers also thought that reality TV made them think they could achieve anything in life. They also believed the shows made them more aware of social issues and causes.

EXPLORE ONLINE

The focus in Chapter Four was the impact of viewing reality television. It also touched upon a study by the Girl Scouts. The Web site below focuses on this study. As you know, every source is different. How is the information given in the Web site different from the information in this chapter? What information is the same? How do the two sources present information differently? What can you learn from this Web site?

Girl Scouts: Real to Me, Tips for Girls
www.girlscouts.org/research/pdf/real_to_me_tip_sheet_girls.pdf

CHAPTER FIVE

Let's Get Real

Is reality TV fake or is it real? Does it matter? Lots of reality shows simply edit reality to make it exciting. They still stay close to the truth, but there are different degrees of reality.

What Is Real?

Joe Millionaire featured construction worker Evan Marriott posing as a millionaire. He promised not to reveal the truth, jumped on a plane, and flew to

Evan Marriott participated in the staged love reality show *Joe Millionaire.*

Placing the Product

Product placement is when a company pays for its product to be used or featured in the media. The Coca-Cola cups sitting on the desks of the *American Idol* judges are there because of product placement. *America's Next Top Model* had 178 product placement occurrences in 26 episodes in 2011. *The Biggest Loser* had a whopping 533 placements in 34 shows.

France to be on a reality show about dating. He was not really going to marry anyone. But in the final show, he proposed to Zora. The couple quickly parted ways after the show. Both participants received $500,000 from the network. Viewers were led to believe that the search for love was real, when it fact it was all for show.

Producers take thousands of hours of film and condense them into one-hour shows. Because of this, editors can pick and choose scenes that help define a character in the program. Characters are made to look good and bad, bright and not so bright, or funny and dull. They become stereotypes.

Big Brother participants are videotaped in the Red Room, and the film is later edited to fit the show.

The cups in front of the *American Idol* judges are part of Coca-Cola's product placement on the show.

In *The Real World*, *Jersey Shore*, and *Big Brother*, producers stage an environment in which entertaining scenes can occur. The environment is separated from other people. A confined space adds fuel to conflicts between the participants.

Dollars and Sense

There are many reasons why reality shows continue to grow in numbers year by year. Reality TV shows are popular with a wide audience. They cost less than $500,000 for an hour-long episode. That's about one-third of the cost for a scripted comedy or drama program. *American Idol* earned almost $900 million in ad sales in 2008. The show's official sponsors

FURTHER EVIDENCE

There is quite a bit of information about reality television in Chapter Five. It covered the work that goes into making a show look real. But if you could pick out the main point of the chapter, what would it be? What evidence was given to support that point? Visit the Web site below to learn more about reality television. Choose a quote from the Web site that relates to this chapter. Does this quote support the author's main point? Does it make a new point? Write a few sentences explaining how the quote you found relates to this chapter.

Unscripted Does Not Mean Unwritten
www.wga.org/organizesub.aspx?id=1096

Some Rules of Reality

In July 2010, an anonymous reality show producer was quoted in the article "20 Behind-the-Scenes Truths of Reality TV" published in *Esquire* magazine. The producer stated that everything in reality TV is mapped out. The cast is not allowed to do anything. They are monitored 24 hours a day. And they barely have contact with friends or family.

(Coca-Cola, AT&T, and Ford) pay $50 to $60 million a year for product placement.

Future Reality

From game shows to makeovers, talent shows to humor, and on into lifestyle reality, a new breed of programs became part of television. Producers and editors carefully craft the shows.

But reality TV shows remain very popular. Audiences don't seem to object if there is a blurring of the line between fact and fiction.

Audiences show their support by texting votes in to save their favorite reality TV participant. They also write about these shows on social media sites such as Facebook and Twitter.

Host Tyra Banks poses with winner Teyona Anderson from the show *America's Next Top Model.*

The cast of *Jersey Shore* is filmed day and night for their show.

The reality of this type of programming is that it is popular, it is cheap to produce, and it makes a lot of money in advertising dollars. Like it or not, reality television, in some form or another, is here to stay.

In an article for the Museum of Broadcast Communications, author Beth Seaton discussed reality television. She wrote:

> *Rather than solely relying upon the use of actual documentary or "live" footage for its credibility, reality programming often draws upon a mix of acting, news footage, interviews and re-creations in a highly simulated pretense towards the "real." . . . And yet, "reality" is dramatized on reality programming to an extent quite unlike conventional television news, and this dramatization is often geared towards more promotional, rather than informational, ends. In essence, the effectivity of reality programs lies in their ability to dramatize "the real" by drawing upon popular memory and forms, specifically the popular forms of commodity culture.*

Source: Beth Seaton. "Reality Programming." Museum of Broadcast Communications. January 12, 2008. Web. Accessed September 21, 2012.

Changing Minds

This text passage discusses whether reality television represents reality or if it is staged. Take a position on this issue. Imagine your best friend has the opposite opinion. Write a short essay trying to change your friend's mind. Make sure you detail your opinion and give your reasons for it. Include facts and details that support your reasons.

IMPORTANT DATES

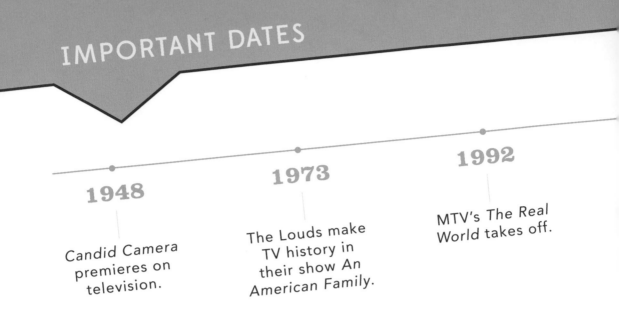

1948

Candid Camera premieres on television.

1973

The Louds make TV history in their show *An American Family*.

1992

MTV's *The Real World* takes off.

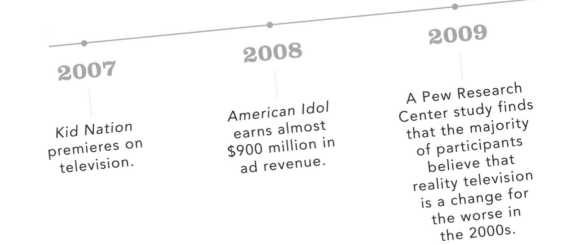

2007

Kid Nation premieres on television.

2008

American Idol earns almost $900 million in ad revenue.

2009

A Pew Research Center study finds that the majority of participants believe that reality television is a change for the worse in the 2000s.

2000

Fifty-one million people watch the first-season finale of *Survivor*.

2002

American Idol is first shown on TV.

2003

Trista Rehn and Ryan Sutter make a love connection that lasts on *The Bachelorette*.

2010

A Brigham Young University study finds that there are 52 acts of aggression per hour on reality TV.

2011

In *America's Next Top Model*, there are 178 product placements in 26 episodes.

2012

Christina Aguilera makes $225,000 per episode of *The Voice*.

Say What?

Studying reality television can mean learning new words. Find five words in this book that you've never seen or heard before. Find out what they mean. Write the meaning in your own words. Now use the words in a new sentence.

Changing Minds

This book discusses the history and evolution of reality TV. It points out the fact that reality TV is often not real and that viewing this type of programming can have a negative impact. Take a position on whether you think reality TV is just harmless entertainment or potentially harmful. Write a short essay detailing your opinion, giving reasons for your opinion as well as facts and details that support those reasons.

Tell the Tale

This book discusses the reality of reality television. Write 200 words that tell the true story of a reality star contestant's experience on a reality show. Include thoughts about how the edited show was different from what really happened. Be sure to set the scene, develop a sequence of events, and offer a conclusion.

Surprise Me

Think about what you have learned from this book. Can you name the two or three facts in this book that you found most surprising? Write a short paragraph about each, describing what you found most surprising and why.

GLOSSARY

confine
to keep within
certain bounds

culture
the ideas, customs,
traditions, and way of life
of a group of people

dialogue
conversation, especially in
a play, movie, television
program, or book

documentary
a movie or television program
about real people and events

eliminate
to remove someone from a
competition by a defeat

genre
certain kind of creative work,
such as a television program

hoard
to collect large amounts of
garbage or objects

interaction
action between people,
groups, or things

participant
person involved with an
event, such as a reality
television program or contest

renovate
to restore something to
good condition

LEARN MORE

Books

Edwards, Posy. *The Kardashians: A Krazy Life.* London: Orion, 2012.

Tieck, Sarah. *Scotty McCreery: American Idol Winner.* Minneapolis, MN: ABDO, 2012.

Woog, Adam. *Reality TV*. Yankton, SD: Erickson Press, 2007.

Web Links

To learn more about reality television, visit ABDO Publishing Company online at **www.abdopublishing.com**. Web sites about reality television are featured on our Book Links page. These links are routinely monitored and updated to provide the most current information available.

Visit **www.mycorelibrary.com** for free additional tools for teachers and students.

INDEX

American Idol, 5, 6, 13–14, 16, 20, 21, 26, 34, 37–38

America's Funniest Home Videos, 22

America's Got Talent, 20, 21

America's Next Top Model, 21, 34

Apprentice, The, 13, 21, 28

Bachelorette, The, 21, 25

Bachelor, The, 21, 25, 28

Big Brother, 8, 14, 20, 36

Biggest Loser, The, 21, 34

Candid Camera, 11–13

Clarkson, Kelly, 16

Cowell, Simon, 13

Dancing with the Stars, 20, 22

DelVecchio, Pauly D, 16

Expedition Robinson, 14

Extreme Makeover: Home Edition, 21

Funt, Allen, 11, 13

genres, 19–23

Hoarders, 8, 22

Jersey Shore, 16, 23, 29, 36

Joe Millionaire, 33–34

Kardashian, Kourtney, 5

Keeping Up with the Kardashians, 5, 22

Kid Nation, 28

Lopez, Jennifer, 5

Marriott, Evan, 33

Medina, Chris, 5

Mesnick, Jason, 25

Real World, The, 6, 13, 36

Rehn, Trista, 25

studies on reality TV, 26, 28–29, 31

Survivor, 6, 14, 20, 26, 28

Sutter, Ryan, 25

Underwood, Carrie, 16, 26

Voice, The, 5, 16, 20

X Factor, 20

ABOUT THE AUTHOR

Megan Kopp is the author of 25 nonfiction books for kids, as well as more than 500 published articles in magazines, newspapers, and online. She admits to the guilty pleasure of watching Survivor and The Amazing Race.

DISCARD